ENGLISH
Practice for
Key Stage 1
National tests

Ages 6-7

TEST
YOUR CHILD
ENGLISH

Reading Booklet pull-out

Test Booklet pull-out

Let's learn at home

ENGLISH

INTRODUCTION

What are the Key Stage 1 National tests?

Every year in May, children in Year 2 who have their seventh birthday between 1st September in the year before and 31st August of the current year take the National tests. They are asked to do two tests, English and Mathematics, which are formally assessed and their teacher assesses their performance in science from the work they have been doing during the year. These assessments are designed to show the levels of work your child is able to achieve in these core subjects. The tests are carried out over one week. The papers are marked by the school and are then sent to external moderators. The final results give parents and teachers an indication of each child's performance in relation to the standards set out in the National Curriculum (NC).

What the test results mean

Your child's National test results will be used by the school to plan future work for your child and make provision for any strengths or weaknesses that the tests may have revealed. The results will also be entered on your child's school records for evidence of the progress she is making through the school.

About the English tests

The tests for English assess basic skills in reading, writing, spelling and handwriting. They consist of:
- an informal reading assessment
- a reading comprehension test
- a writing test, including a handwriting test
- a spelling test.

Using this book

Before your child attempts the written tests, you need to assess her reading using the Informal Reading Assessment on pages 3–4. If you assess your child's reading to be at Level 1 or below, it is not recommended that she attempts the Level 2 Reading Comprehension test at this time. If you assess your child's reading at Level 2C or above, she may attempt the Level 2 Reading Comprehension test on pages 3–19 of the pull-out Reading booklet. The Level 3 Reading Comprehension test is for children who achieve Level 2A in both the Informal Reading Assessment and the Level 2 Reading Comprehension test.

Children at Levels 1–3 may attempt the Writing test on pages 1–4 of the Test Booklet, as this test is assessed by outcome (that is, you will make an assessment of the writing as matched against a set of criteria outlined on pages 7–8).

If you assess your child's writing to be at Level 2C or above, follow on with the Spelling test on pages 7–11 of the Test Booklet.

Once the Informal Reading Assessment is completed, the written tests may be taken at any time, as suits you and your child. It is not necessary or desirable that the tests follow each other too closely. Space them out over a period of time.

The Informal Reading Assessment

The Informal Reading Assessment helps you to assess how accurately and fluently your child can read aloud. It helps you to assess how well your child understands what she reads and how she responds to a story by discussing plot, characters and story setting, and developments that might follow on from it. Assessing how well a child reads aloud is a complex skill and one that teachers develop with training and experience. However, there are defined criteria which will help you, as a parent.or carer, to arrive at an informal overall assessment (see page 4).

In school, the reading assessment follows the same structure for each Level at Key Stage 1. The test material sent to schools includes a list of book titles for Levels 1 and 2 from which the school chooses a selection for use with the children. The notes accompanying the test material emphasize that the books chosen must not have been seen by the children before the assessment. The books are carefully selected to conform to particular criteria such as a clear storyline, interesting settings and characters, language and vocabulary likely to be familiar to Key Stage 1 children, and good quality illustrations.

Assessing reading informally at home

Selecting the books
To make the home assessment similar to the school one, choose three or four children's story books that your child has not read. The books could be chosen from your local library, from the school or class library, or from friends or relatives. Alternatively, a good bookshop should have a selection of current children's books.

The chosen books should be at a similar level to the books your child is using at school, as far as you can judge. If in doubt, your child's teacher, the local librarian, or a bookshop assistant may be able to suggest suitable books. When you are selecting books, look for:
- an interesting story in a setting that is familiar to your child or that extends her experience
- a clear storyline and story structure (a beginning, a middle and a conclusion)
- a story that has repetitive patterns of language, perhaps with some rhyme and rhythm
- good illustrations that support or add to the story
- pages that are well set out with not too much text on each page and with a good balance between print and illustration
- clear print of an appropriate size for your child's age group.

Choosing a book
Show the selected three or four books to your child and encourage her to look through them. Allow her to choose the one she would like to read. Ask why she chose that particular book: was it the illustrations she liked, or the cover, for example? Ask whether she has read other similar books, or books by the same author.

Making your initial assessment
By discussing the chosen book with your child, you will be able to judge whether she has basic knowledge about print, and whether she is able to read any letters and words rather than using only the pictures. Can your child say what the book appears to be about by flicking through the pages? Can she comment on the use of capital letters in the title, or find the name of the author and talk about other books the author has written? Can your child recognize words or letters in the title without being prompted?

Assessing your child's reading
Ask your child to find the place where the story begins. Explain that you are going to read the story together and that you will give help if necessary. Let your child take over the reading if she can do so. Help her with words she finds difficult by pointing out the initial letter sound or by telling her the whole word.

Read as much of the story as you need to make your assessment. During the reading, your child may want to comment on what is happening in the story. Just after the reading, use this checklist to assess what strategies your child is using to read the story.

- recognizes frequently used words such as 'and', 'the' and so on
- uses initial letters to work out words in the context of the sentence
- understands the sense of what is being read
- uses punctuation such as full stops and commas to give meaning to reading
- comments on what is happening in the story
- follows the words accurately by pointing and turning the page at the right time
- uses knowledge of rhyme to read unfamiliar words.

Finishing the assessment

Talk about the book with your child. Find out which parts she liked and why. Does she know what happens next? Ask what she thought about the style and content of the pictures and whether the illustrations helped with reading the story.

Assessing the level of your child's reading

Use your observations of your child's reading and how she responded to the book to match against the level descriptors given below. Bear in mind, though, that an informal assessment can only give an informal result.

Level descriptions for Informal Reading Assessment

LEVEL W
Your child may appear to be unaware of the significance of the information given on the covers of the book, the purpose of the print and pictures and so on. However, she may be able to talk about the story when you read it together and point to or recognize some of the letters or a name in the story.

LEVEL 1
Your child should be willing and keen to choose a book and discuss the various items to be found on the cover. She should have some knowledge of letter names and sounds and be able to use this knowledge to work out words. She should know where the story begins and be able to read a small number of familiar words. When asked about the story, she should be able to say which parts she liked and found interesting.

LEVEL 2
Level 2 is the level that the majority of children aged seven achieve. It is divided into three grades: Level 2A (highest), 2B and 2C, because it encompasses a wide range of performance.

At **Level 2C**, a child uses one or two of the reading strategies listed above. She should be able to read most of the story accurately by herself. The reading may be hesitant, going from word to word, and your child may need to pause in the reading to make sure she understands what is happening. After reading, your child may be able to talk about the most obvious points, relying on the pictures for most of her information.

At **Level 2B**, your child uses three or four of the strategies above. The reading is almost fully accurate and she makes use of full stops and commas. She realizes when the reading does not make sense and will correct herself. Your child can discuss the story more fully by talking about the setting and how the story developed.

At **Level 2A**, your child uses five to seven of the strategies above. The reading of the story is accurate. With encouragement, she will try to work out words she doesn't know. She reads confidently and with expression. After the reading, your child is able to discuss the story with full understanding about the events and the characters.

LEVEL 3
Your child uses all the reading strategies listed above and reads with pace and fluency by herself, shows full understanding of the story and discusses the book with insight afterwards.

Parent's
Booklet

The Reading Comprehension test

There is no time-limit for the Reading test, but for most children 45 minutes is long enough. This test need not be completed all at once and your child may have a break. (This can best be taken between the story and the information section.)

Marking the test

Pages 5–7 give suggested answers and marking guidelines. Discuss your child's answers with her as you mark the paper. If she did not answer a question at all, encourage her to explain why, and discuss any problems. Try not to be inflexible about 'right or 'wrong' answers. The answers given are suggested guidelines only and you need to make allowances for the different ways individuals express themselves.

● In the margin of the test paper, write the number of marks scored by your child in the mark box alongside each question. If your child gets the answer wrong, put '0' in the box. If your child does not attempt the question, put a '–' in the box. Do not leave any mark box empty.

● Add up the number of marks scored on each page using the 'total' box in the bottom right-hand corner. Transfer the total marks to the grid on the inside back cover of this book.

ANSWERS TO LEVEL 2 READING COMPREHENSION TEST
The Sweet Porridge by Wanda Gág

Answers to pages 4–10 (Reading Booklet)

Question	Answer	Mark
A	in a little village	practice
B	They were very poor.	practice
1	to find some nuts or berries	1
2	She gave her a little cooking kettle.	1
3	on the stove	1
4	The kettle would cook some porridge.	1
5	the girl	1
6	They could eat all the porridge they wanted.	1
7	She asked the kettle to make some porridge.	1
8	She had forgotten the right words.	1
9	The kettle kept on cooking.	1
10	It filled with porridge.	1
11	to escape from the porridge	1
12	● They were surprised/frightened/worried. ● They didn't know what to do.	1
13	She stopped the kettle.	1
14	Possible answers could be along the lines of: ● I think they would use the kettle again if the girl was there. ● They would use the kettle again because they needed it for food. ● They would use it again because they had no money. Or: ● I don't think they would use the kettle in case it went wrong again. ● The people in the village may not like them to use it because it went wrong before.	1

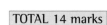
TOTAL 14 marks

Parent's
Booklet

Cereals

Answers to pages 11–19

Question	Answer	Mark
A	cereals	practice
B	for breakfast	practice
15	the seeds	1
16	● They were easy to grow.	
	● They gave people a lot of food.	1
17	rain	1
18	the goddess of grain	1
19	mild	1
20	It would not get ripe.	1
21	oats	1
22	● because the weather is mild	
	● because it rains a lot	
	● because they grow well in this country	1
23	millet	1
24	● It grows where other crops can't grow.	
	● It gets ripe quickly.	1
25	two or three	1
26	Some people there hardly eat anything else.	1
27	oats	1
28	2 cups	1
29	● It would not be very sweet.	
	● It would not taste so nice.	1
30	when it is thick	1

TOTAL 16 marks

ANSWERS TO LEVEL 3 READING COMPREHENSION TEST

How the Polar Bear Became by Ted Hughes

Answers to pages 13–16 (Test Booklet)

Question	Answer	Mark
A	They admired each other.	practice
B	● They wanted to be admired.	
	● They wanted to win the contest.	practice
1	● She might get muddy.	
	● Her fur might get splashed.	1
2	There was too much dust and dirt.	1
3	They made her feel happy/proud/special/beautiful.	1
4	● Because they never won the contest.	
	● Because they were not white.	1
5	● He was a great traveller.	
	● He had been to every country in the world.	1
6	● It was very clean.	
	● There was no dust or dirt.	
	● It was all white.	
	● She could be queen.	
	● There were no crowds.	1

6

Reading Booklet

First name

Last name

Instructions for parents

Before the test

First make sure your child feels happy and relaxed about doing the test, and explain that it will help her when she comes to do similar tests at school. Ensure your child has a pen or pencil and an eraser. Explain that you will give her help for the first page, but after that she will be working on her own. If your child gets stuck on a question, she should go on and try the rest of the questions. When your child has finished, she can go back to check through her work and try to fill in any answers she has left out.

Starting the test

Look through the different sections of the Level 2 test with your child. Read the first section, 'The Sweet Porridge', together, and go to the practice questions. Read the first question and ask your child to decide on the best answer and tick the box. Read the second question and point out that she should write the answer on the line. Explain to your child that she can look back at the passage to check her answers and change some, if necessary, by crossing them out or erasing them. Tell your child the rest of the test must be completed without help from you and that if she gets stuck on a question, to go on to the next one. Any gaps can be filled in at the end of the test.

During the test

After helping your child with reading and answering the practice questions for the Level 2 test, do not give any further help with the reading. Resist giving your child any clues which would help her answer any of the questions or prompt her in any way.

Level 2 Reading Comprehension Test

Second Helpings

MARKING GRID		
Page	Marks possible	Marks scored
5	3	
6–7	5	
8–9	4	
10	2	
12–13	4	
14–15	4	
16–17	4	
19	4	
TOTAL	30	

First name

Last name

The Sweet Porridge

by Wanda Gág

Once there was a poor but worthy girl who lived with her mother in a little village. They were so poor, these two, that many a night they had to go hungry to bed, and at last there came a time when there was nothing left in the house for them to eat.

Practice questions

A. Where did the mother and girl live?

☐ in a little village   ☐ in the woods

☐ in the town   ☐ by a river

B. Why were the mother and girl so hungry?

_____

Now the girl, hoping perhaps to find some nuts or berries, went out into the woods, where she met an old woman. Strangely enough, the woman already knew that the two were in trouble and, handing the girl a little cooking kettle, she said, "Take this, my child."

1. Why did the girl go into the woods?

☐ to meet an old woman

☐ to find some nuts or berries

☐ to pick some flowers

☐ to go for a walk

2. What did the old woman give the girl?

_____

"If you set it on the stove and say to it, 'Cook, little kettle, cook,' it will start bubbling and boiling and will cook up a mess of good, sweet millet porridge for you and your mother. Then, when you have eaten your fill, you need only to say, 'Stop, little kettle, stop,' and it will stop cooking until the next time."

3. Where did the woman tell the girl to put the little kettle?

☐ on the floor   ☐ on the bed

☐ on the stove   ☐ on the table

4. What would happen if the girl said, "Cook, little kettle, cook"?

_____

And that was the way it turned out to be. The girl took the kettle home to her mother, and now the two could eat all the sweet porridge they wanted and were never hungry any more.

5. Who took the little kettle home?

☐ the girl   ☐ the mother

☐ the woman   ☐ the cook

6. Why were the girl and her mother never hungry?

☐ The woman gave them food.

☐ They could eat all the porridge they wanted.

☐ They could buy enough food.

☐ They went to live with a friend.

One day the girl went away for a few hours and the mother, feeling hungry, said, "Cook, little kettle, cook." Immediately a good hearty smell filled the kitchen, the kettle began to cook, and soon the mother was enjoying a big bowl of good, sweet porridge. But when she had eaten her fill and wanted to make the kettle stop cooking, she found she had forgotten the right words.

7. What did the mother do when she was hungry after the girl had gone?

_____

_____

7

1 mark

8. What had the mother forgotten?

_____

8

1 mark

So the little kettle kept on cooking – cooked and cooked until the porridge rose over the rim of the kettle. Cooked and cooked some more until it flowed all over the stove. Cooked and cooked and kept on cooking until the little cottage was filled with porridge. Cooked and cooked until it poured out of the windows into the street, and then into all the huts and cottages along the way.

9. What did the little kettle do?

9

1 mark

_____

_____

10. What happened to the little cottage?

10

1 mark

☐ It fell down.   ☐ The doors shut tight.

☐ It set on fire.   ☐ It filled with porridge.

At this the people ran from their houses to
escape from the bubbling, boiling flood, but
the porridge cooked merrily on until it had
filled the whole village. Even then it didn't
stop but spread out over the fields, flowing in
all directions as though it were trying to feed
the whole world. Everyone was worried, but
no one knew what to do.

11. Why did the people run from their houses?

_____

12. How do you think the people felt when they saw
the porridge?

_____

_____

At last, when only one little hut was left unfilled with porridge, the girl returned. When she saw what had happened, she quickly cried, "Stop, little kettle, stop!" And of course the kettle obeyed and stopped cooking – but the only way the village folk could return to their houses was to eat their way through the porridge!

13. What happened when the girl came home?

☐ She ran into the house.

☐ She stopped the kettle.

☐ She went away again.

☐ Her mother was cross with her.

14. Do you think the mother and girl will use the kettle again?

_____

Why do you think that?

_____

_____

_____

Introduction

The story you have just read is about a magic
kettle that makes millet porridge. In the story
a kettle is another name for a cooking pot.
Millet comes from a cereal plant. In the next
part of the booklet you will read about
different kinds of cereals, where they are
grown and how they are used.

At the end of the booklet you will find a
recipe for making porridge. You may like to try
it for your breakfast one day.

Practice questions

A. What is the next part of the booklet about?

☐ porridge   ☐ a kettle

☐ millet   ☐ cereals

B. When would you usually eat porridge?

Cereals

Cereals are plants that belong to the grass
family. The seeds of these plants are hard
grains that can be eaten. Cereals were the
first plants to be grown for food. The first crops
were grown nearly 15,000 years ago. They
were good crops to use because they gave the
people a lot of food and they were easy to
grow.

15. Which part of a cereal plant can be eaten?

| | the roots | | the seeds |

| | the leaves | | the stalk |

16. Why were cereals good crops to grow?

_____

_____

The word cereal comes from a Roman godess called Ceres. She was the godess of grain. The Romans used to hold 'cerealia' festivals each year to make sure there would be plenty of rain to make the crops good.

17. What sort of weather did the cerealia festivals bring?

☐ rain   ☐ fog

☐ wind   ☐ sun

18. Who was Ceres?

17

1 mark

18

1 mark

Total

Pages 12–13

Each cereal grows best in different parts of the world. Some cereals grow where the weather is cool and wet. Other cereals grow where it is hot and dry.

Wheat

Wheat grows best where the weather is mild – not too hot and not too cold. The crop needs cool wet days to start it growing well. When it has grown, it needs sunny days to make the seeds ripe for harvesting. Wheat can be used to make bread.

19. What is the weather like where wheat grows best?

☐ hot   ☐ dry

☐ icy   ☐ mild

20. What would happen if there were no sunny days when the wheat had finished growing?

_____

_____

19

1 mark

20

1 mark

Oats

Oats can grow in a colder climate than wheat.
Like wheat, oats need rain to make the crop
grow. Scotland is a good place to grow them in
this country. Oats can be used to make
porridge, oatcakes and scones. They have
been grown as a crop in this country for more
than 700 years.

21. Which crop grows well in Scotland?

☐ wheat ☐ oats

☐ millet ☐ rice

22. Why do you think oats are grown in this country?

21

1 mark

22

1 mark

Total

Millet

Millet will grow where the weather is hot and dry. It will grow in poor soil. The hot weather ripens the millet grains very quickly. Millet will grow in places where other crops can hardly be grown at all. This makes up for the fact that the crops are not very plentiful.

23. Which crop will grow in poor soil?

23

1 mark

▢ wheat   ▢ millet

▢ rice   ▢ oats

24. What is a good thing about growing millet?

24

1 mark

_____

_____

ENGLISH
Practice for
Key Stage 1
national tests

Ages 6-7

Writing Test

Let's learn at home

ENGLISH

First name	

Last name	

Writing test instructions

1. Choosing a subject to write about

Start by choosing a familiar, favourite book with your child. This could be either a story book or an information book.

Discuss some different writing tasks with your child, based on the book. Some suggestions are:

● writing a letter – this could be to the author of the book, to the illustrator, to a particular character in the story, or a letter from one character to another

● writing about an opinion your child may have formed – this could be about an idea or action in the story that she may agree or disagree with

● writing a review of the book for the use of other children who may be thinking of reading the book

● writing an episode for the story that could follow on from the ending

● writing about an event or incident that your child has personal experience of that may be related to the story in the book in some way

● writing the instructions for making something that may have figured in the book, such as a model or a recipe for something to eat.

2. Planning the writing

When your child has decided what to write about, help her to think about and plan her writing. Use a piece of scrap paper to do this.

If your child is planning to write a **story**, she should consider:
- the characters and what they would be like
- the setting for the story
- the beginning
- the central event of the plot
- the ending.

If your child is planning to write an **information piece** about her opinions, or writing a review, she should think about the points she wants to make, which order they should go in to be logical, and think of reasons for them.

If your child is planning to write a **letter**, she should also include an address (full postal) and use a conventional opening ('Dear…') and ending ('Yours…').

3. Writing the piece

Once your child is happy with the plan, give her some lined paper and a reliable pen or sharp pencil to write the piece. Explain how long she will have to do the writing (this should be no longer than an hour). A reminder about the need for good handwriting and careful spelling would not go amiss.

Then leave your child undisturbed to complete the writing task without further help. After completing the writing, she should read it through and change anything she thinks could be improved such as spelling, vocabulary and punctuation.

4. The handwriting test

When your child is happy with her writing, ask her to copy out one or two of the sentences in her best handwriting. If you prefer, you and your child together can select sentences from your chosen book.

Your child's copied sentences are used as a part of the overall assessment of her writing.

5. Assessing your child's writing

Use the Writing Level indicators on page 8 of the parent's booklet to assess your child's writing. List the points you find about her writing and compare them with the indicators to find the best match. Do the same with the handwriting sentences and compare your points with the examples of handwriting given on pages 9–10.

Spelling test instructions

Make sure your child has a reliable pen or a sharp
pencil and an eraser. Explain that you will be able to
help her at the beginning of the test, but after that she
will be working on her own. If your child thinks she has
made a mistake, she can cross out the word if she is
using a pen, or rub it out if she is using a pencil, and
have another try. Point out that some of the words are
easy to spell and some of them are harder, but she
should have a go at them and write the first letter or
letters of the word and any other letters or sounds she
thinks would be correct.

Part 1: the picture test

In the first part of the test your child has to write the
words for the pictures in the boxes below them. The first
word is for practice to make sure your child knows what
she is supposed to do. Ask your child to say what the
practice picture shows and then ask her to write the
word 'tap' in the box below the picture. Check if your
child has been able to do this and tell her what letters
spell the word. When you are sure your child knows
what is expected of her, carry on with the test.

Look at the big picture of the kitchen together and talk
about what is shown in it. Then draw your child's
attention to the small pictures with the boxes below
them around the main picture. Make sure she knows
what each item is. (The target words for this part of the
test are: **bowl, chair, clock, dog, plate, ball, glass, jar,
door, spoon.**)

Next, ask your child to write in the word for the first picture. Tell her that if she is not sure how to spell the word, she should have a try and write in the first letter and any other letters she thinks would be in the word. Remind your child that if she wishes to change a spelling, she can cross or rub it out and have another try. If your child makes a mistake about what any of the pictures represent, tell her what they are.

When your child has finished all the words around the picture, she might like a break before going on to the next part of the test.

Part 2: the dictation

Tell your child you are going to read her a short story. Explain that there is no need to write anything yet, just to listen carefully to the story. At this point, read the dictation passage to your child.

Next, ask your child to look at the version she has in the booklet. Point out that it is the same story but that some of the words are missing. Tell your child you are going to read the story again and when there is a space, you will tell her the word to write in it. Remind your child that she should have a go if she is not sure of the word by putting in the first letter and any other letters she thinks would look right. If your child wants to change a spelling, she can do so.

Read the first sentence slowly and make sure that your child has understood that she should have written the word 'her' in the first space. Continue reading the rest of the story, pausing long enough at each target word in bold for your child to write the word in the space provided. Repeat any word she hasn't heard correctly. Read each target word as clearly as you can so that your child can hear the sounds that make up the word.

Spelling Test

Practice question

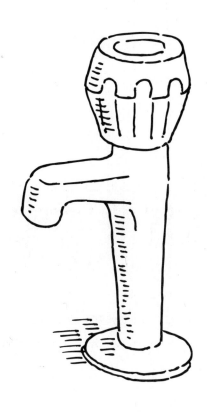

First name

Last name

Breakfast at the farm

8

9

The farm visit

Rose and _____ younger

_____, Tim, live on a _____.

They go to _____ in the nearby

_____. Every _____, the

headteacher arranges with Rose and Tim's dad,

Mr Green, for a class visit.

The children always _____ their

visit. There are young lambs and calves to see,

and Mr Green lets them _____ the

young animals with bottles of milk. The children

can have rides on the _____ donkeys

and give them pieces of apple and carrot.

There is an _____ tractor in the

yard, and the children love to climb on it and

pretend to _____ it. Mr Green will not

allow them to climb the hay bales stacked in the

barn _____ it is too dangerous. The

bales may _____ and hurt the children

or there may be _____ tools hidden in

the bales that _____ injure them.

Mr Green shows the children all the machinery

he uses for harvesting the _____. He

explains how they work and tells them

_____ how the crops were harvested in

days gone by.

_____ it is time to leave, Mrs Green

gives _____ child a small

_____ she has _____. The

flour she used was from the wheat they had grown

last year.

Level 3 Reading Comprehension Test

The Ways of a Polar Bear

MARKING GRID		
Page	Marks possible	Marks scored
14–15	7	
16–17	7	
18–19	8	
TOTAL	22	

First name

Last name

How the Polar Bear Became by Ted Hughes

Practice questions

A. What did the animals do when they grew tired of admiring the trees, the flowers and the sun?

☐ They went to sleep.

☐ They played games.

☐ They admired each other.

☐ They looked for something to eat.

B. Why do you think the animals tried hard to look beautiful?

_____

_____

(These questions are for pages 23–25 of the Reading booklet.)

1. Why didn't Polar Bear want to go out in the wet?

_____

_____

1

1 mark

2. Polar Bear wanted to go to another country. What didn't she like about where she lived?

☐ It was too hot.

☐ There was too much dust and dirt.

☐ She didn't like the Seals.

☐ There was nothing to eat.

2

1 mark

3. How did the young Seals make Polar Bear feel?

_____

_____

3

1 mark

4. Why did most of the animals give up trying to make themselves beautiful?

_____

_____

4

1 mark

(pages 26–27)

5. How did Peregrine Falcon know about other countries of the world?

_____

_____

5

1 mark

6. Why did Peregrine Falcon think Polar Bear would want to go to the country he told her about?

_____

_____

6

1 mark

7. Who went to the new country with Polar Bear?

_____

_____

7

1 mark

Total

Pages 14–15

(page 28)

8. How do you think Peregrine Falcon felt about Little Brown Mouse winning the beauty contest?

8

1 mark

_____

_____

(the whole story)

9. Why was Polar Bear thought to be so beautiful?

9

1 mark

_____

10. Do you think the animals were pleased with Peregrine Falcon?

☐ Yes   ☐ No

Why?

10

1 mark

_____

_____

11. How do you think the animals felt after Polar Bear had gone?

☐   They were upset and sorry.

☐   They were happy and glad.

☐   They wished they could have gone too.

☐   They were glad Peregrine Falcon came back.

11

1 mark

The Arctic

(page 29)

12. What part of the world did Peregrine Falcon tell Polar Bear about?

_____

_____

13. How did the Arctic get its name?

☐ from the ice

☐ from the snow

☐ from a group of stars

☐ from Peregrine Falcon

(pages 30–31)

14. Where is the only place in the world you would find polar bears?

_____

_____

Level 3
Reading
test

15. What would happen if polar bears didn't have thick fur coats and layers of fat under their skin?

☐ They wouldn't be able to swim.

☐ They would freeze to death.

☐ They would eat more food.

☐ They wouldn't be able to hunt.

15

1 mark

16. What is good about the colour of the polar bear's coat?

_____

_____

16

1 mark

17. Who came to the Arctic from Asia?

☐ the polar bears

☐ Roald Amundsen

☐ Adolf Nordenskjöld

☐ the Eskimos

17

1 mark

18. What do you think it would be like to live in the Arctic?

_____

_____

_____

18

1 mark

19. What is the Arctic ocean like?

_____

_____

19

1 mark

20. What are the names of the two sea routes the explorers found?

_____

_____

20

2 marks

21. Why are polar bears able to live in the Arctic?

☐ They are very big.

☐ They are strong swimmers.

☐ They can do very high dives.

☐ They have thick coats and layers of fat.

21

1 mark

Total

Pages 18–19

Rice

Rice grows best where the weather is warm. It is grown in fields that are flooded with water. These fields are called 'paddies'. It is an important crop in Asia where some people hardly eat anything but rice. The rice crop grows quickly and the farmers can grow two or three crops every year. Over half the population of the world eats rice as their main food.

25. How many crops of rice can a farmer grow each year?

☐ nine or ten   ☐ five or six

☐ two or three   ☐ seven or eight

26. Why is so much rice needed in Asia?

_____

In this part of the world, porridge is made from the grains of oats. The oat grains have been rolled flat in a mill so that they are like flakes. They are called 'rolled oats'. Porridge makes a good hot breakfast for a cold winter morning.

Recipe

Porridge for two helpings

1 cup of porridge oats
2 cups of water or milk

1. Measure out the oats and put them in a pan.

2. Measure out the milk or water and mix it with the oats.

3. Cook gently over a medium heat. Keep stirring the porridge until it is thick and cooked.

4. Serve the porridge in a bowl with milk. Add sugar or honey to make it sweet.

5. Eat it while it's hot!

27. Which cereal is used in the recipe for making porridge?

☐ millet   ☐ wheat

☐ rice   ☐ oats

28. How much milk or water do you need?

_____

29. What would the porridge be like without adding sugar or honey?

_____

30. When is the porridge cooked?

☐ when it is runny

☐ when the oats are mixed with the water

☐ when the oats are put in the pan

☐ when it is thick

Let's learn at home
ENGLISH

Reading
Booklet

27

1 mark

28

1 mark

29

1 mark

30

1 mark

Total

Page 19

Level 3 Reading Comprehension

The Ways of a Polar Bear

Contents

Introduction

The story you are about to read was written by Ted Hughes. In the story he tells you about how he thinks polar bears came to live where they do. He has written many stories about animals. He imagined how each animal came to be and why they look as they do. Some of his stories are poems.

How the Polar Bear Became

by Ted Hughes

When the animals had been on earth for some time they grew tired of admiring the trees, the flowers and the sun. They began to admire each other. Every animal was eager to be admired, and spent a part of each day making itself look more beautiful.

Soon they began to hold beauty contests.

Sometimes Tiger won the prize, sometimes Eagle, and sometimes Ladybird. Every animal tried hard.

One animal in particular won the prize almost every time. This was Polar Bear.

Polar Bear was white. Not quite snowy white, but much whiter than any of the other creatures. Everyone admired her. In secret, too, everyone was envious of her. But however much they wished that she wasn't quite so beautiful, they couldn't help giving her the prize.

"Polar Bear, " they said, "with your white fur, you are almost too beautiful."

All this went to Polar Bear's head. In fact, she became vain. She was always washing

and polishing her fur, trying to make it still whiter. After a while she was winning the prize every time. The only times any other creature got a chance to win was when it rained. On those days Polar Bear would say:

"I shall not go out in the wet. The other creatures will be muddy, and my white fur may get splashed."

Then, perhaps, Frog or Duck would win for a change.

She had a crowd of young admirers who were always hanging around her cave. They were mainly Seals, all very giddy. Whenever she came out they made a loud shrieking roar:

"Ooooooh! How beautiful she is!"

Before long, her white fur was more important to Polar Bear than anything. Whenever a single speck of dust landed on the tip of one hair of it – she was furious.

"How can I be expected to keep beautiful in this country!" she cried then. "None of you have ever seen me at my best, because of the dirt here. I am really much whiter than any of you have ever seen me. I think I shall have to go into another country. A country where there

is none of this dust. Which country would be best?"

She used to talk in this way because then the Seals would cry:

"Oh, please don't leave us. Please don't take your beauty away from us. We will do anything for you."

And she loved to hear this.

Soon animals were coming from all over the world to look at her. They stared and stared as Polar Bear stretched out on her rock in the sun. Then they went off home and tried to make themselves look like her. But it was no use. They were all the wrong colour. They were black, or brown, or yellow, or ginger, or fawn, or speckled, but not one of them was white. Soon most of them gave up trying to look beautiful. But they still came every day to gaze enviously at Polar Bear. Some brought picnics. They sat in a vast crowd among the trees in front of her cave.

"Just look at her, " said Mother Hippo to her children. "Now see that you grow up like that."

But nothing pleased Polar Bear.

"The dust these crowds raise!" she sighed.
"Why can't I ever get away from them? If only
there were some spotless, shining country, all
for me…"

Now pretty well all the creatures were tired
of her being so much more admired than they
were. But one creature more so than the rest.
He was Peregrine Falcon.

He was a beautiful bird, all right. But he was
not white. Time and again in the beauty
contests he was runner-up to Polar Bear.

"If it were not for her," he raged to himself, "I
should be first every time."

He thought and thought for a plan to get rid
of her. How? How? How? At last he had it.

One day he went up to Polar Bear.

Now Peregrine Falcon had been to every
country in the world. He was a great traveller,
as all the creatures well knew.

"I know a country," he said to Polar Bear,
"which is so clean it is even whiter than you
are. Yes, yes, I know, you are beautifully white,

but this country is even whiter. The rocks are clear glass and the earth is frozen ice-cream. There is no dirt there, no dust, no mud. You would become whiter than ever in that country. And no one lives there. You could be queen of it.

Polar Bear tried to hide her excitement.

"I could be queen of it, you say?" she cried. "This country sounds made for me. No crowds, no dirt? And the rocks, you say, are glass?"

"The rocks," said Peregrine Falcon, "are mirrors."

"Wonderful!" cried Polar Bear.

"And the rain," he said, "is white face powder."

"Better than ever!" she cried. "How quickly can I be there, away from all these staring crowds and all this dirt?"

"I am going to another country," she told the other animals. "It is too dirty here to live."

Peregrine Falcon hired Whale to carry his passenger. He sat on Whale's forehead, calling out the directions. Polar Bear sat on the shoulder, gazing at the sea. The Seals, who had begged to go with her, sat on the tail.

After some days, they came to the North Pole, where it is all snow and ice.

"Here you are," cried Peregrine Falcon. Everthing is just as I said. No crowds, no dirt, nothing but beautiful clean whiteness."

"And the rocks actually are mirrors!" cried

Polar Bear, and she ran to the nearest iceberg to repair her beauty after the long trip.

Every day now, she sat on one iceberg or another, making herself beautiful in the mirror of the ice. Always, near her, sat the Seals. Her fur became whiter and whiter in this new clean country. And as it became whiter, the Seals praised her beauty more and more. When she herself saw the improvement in her looks she said:

"I shall never go back to that dirty old country again."

And there she is still, with all her admirers around her.

Peregrine Falcon flew back to the other creatures and told them that Polar Bear had gone for ever. They were all very glad, and set about making themselves beautiful at once. Every single one was saying to himself:

"Now that Polar Bear is out of the way, perhaps I shall have a chance of the prize at the beauty contest."

And Peregrine Falcon was saying to himself:

"Surely, now, I am the most beautiful of all creatures."

But that first contest was won by Little Brown Mouse for her pink feet.

Now read about the polar bear's homeland – what it is like and who discovered it.

The Arctic

The place Peregrine Falcon described to Polar Bear was the Arctic. The Arctic is an ocean at the top of the world and it surrounds the North Pole. It is so very cold there that most of the ocean has frozen solid into a huge island of floating ice. This island of ice is surrounded by permanently frozen land. The Arctic is the part of the world between the North Pole and the northern tree line. This tree line circles the top of the world. Inside the line, towards the North Pole, the climate is too cold for any tree to grow. The Arctic is named after the group of stars called The Great Bear. 'Arktos' is the greek word for 'bear'.

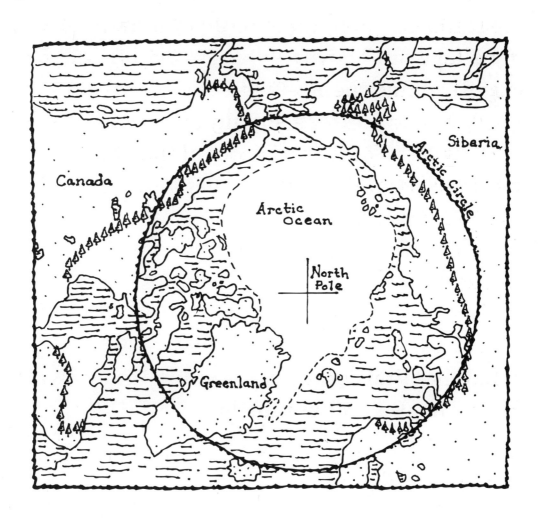

The Polar Bear

Life in such a very cold place is too hard for most creatures. Polar bears are one of the few creatures that are able to live there. In fact, polar bears are not found anywhere else in the world. Among the other animals that live in the Arctic are seals and walruses. These are the animals the polar bears hunt for food.

The polar bears live on the floating ice. Their white coats act as a camouflage against the ice and snow. Their thick coats of fur and the layers of fat under their skins keep the polar bears warm in the freezing temperatures of the Arctic.

Polar bears are the largest animals in the Arctic. When they are fully grown, they can weigh as much as six adult people.

They are expert swimmers and divers. They swim slowly for days at a time using their front legs. Their back legs act as a rudder. They can dive more than 15 metres from the top of an iceberg into the icy water.

Polar bears are clever hunters. They wait on the ice by a seal's air hole. As soon as the seal comes up for air, the polar bear pounces. It kills the seal with a blow from its huge paw and a bite at the back of the seal's head. Most of the food a polar bear eats is seal meat.

Exploring the Arctic

The earliest people to explore and live in the Arctic came from Asia. They were the ancestors of the present day Inuit people who used to be called Eskimos.

Much later, at the beginning of the 16th century, English and Dutch seamen began to search the north for a quicker way to get to China and India. These were the countries where they could buy silk and spices to sell at home. They wanted to find a way over the top of the world.

Going south round the Cape of Good Hope and Cape Horn took a long time. There was also the risk of attack by boats from Spain and Portugal. The explorers searched for a northern sea route which would take them through the Arctic ocean.

After nearly 400 years of people trying, an explorer from Sweden called Adolf Nordenskjöld found the north-east passage by sailing along the Siberian coast. Four years later in 1905, the Norwegian explorer Roald Amundsen found a way through the north-west passage by sailing along the north coast of America.

Exploring and finding the sea routes helped to bring people and trade to the Arctic.

Reading
Booklet

Acknowledgements

Faber and Faber Limited for the use of 'The Sweet Porridge' by Wanda Gág from *More Tales from Grimm* © 1947, The Estate of Wanda Gág (1947, Faber and Faber) and 'How the Polar Bear Became' by Ted Hughes from *How the Whale Became and Other Stories* © 1989, Ted Hughes (1989, Faber and Faber).

7	the Seals, Peregrine Falcon and Whale	1
8	He must have been cross/angry/disappointed/shocked.	1
9	She had white fur.	1
10	Possible answers could be along the lines of:	
	● Yes, because they might be able to win the contest.	
	● Yes – they were tired of Polar Bear always winning.	1
11	They were happy and glad.	1

TOTAL 11 marks

The Arctic
Answers to pages 17–19

Question	Answer	Mark
12	the Arctic	1
13	from a group of stars	1
14	the Arctic	1
15	They would freeze to death.	1
16	● It is a camouflage/makes the polar bears hard to see.	1
17	the Eskimos	1
18	Possible answers could be along the lines of:	
	● It would be very cold.	
	● There would only be fish to eat.	
	● Nothing will grow so there wouldn't be much food.	1
19	It is a huge floating island of ice.	1
20	the north-west passage and the north-east passage	2
21	They have thick coats and layers of fat.	1

TOTAL 11 marks

THE WRITING TEST

Follow the instructions given on pages 2–4 of the Test Booklet. The Writing test should last no longer than an hour.

The purpose of the Writing test is to assess how well your child can impart meaning to communicate with the reader. It also indicates the level of your child's understanding, and accurate use of spelling, punctuation and handwriting.

As with the reading, your assessment will be an informal one. It is difficult to judge a child's performance when it is in isolation at home and it cannot be compared with other children's writing. However, there are a number of criteria which may help to establish the possible level of your child's writing.

Assessing the Writing test

When trying to decide which level of performance your child is at you will need to refer carefully to the level descriptors on page 8. After considering the content of the story, the use of punctuation and legibility of the handwriting, find the level that best matches your child's performance. This is not an easy task and you will need to read the criteria for the level above and below that which you think best matches your child. The criteria are all of equal importance and often you will find your child shows some of the characteristics from the level above and some from the level below. This should not be regarded as a problem and you can still arrive at the best match even when some criteria for a level are not shown in your child's writing.

Writing Level indicators

LEVEL W

Writing at this level has single letters or groups of letters to represent words and phrases. The letters show some control over their size and shape. Your child will able to say what the writing means, and read it back to you.

LEVEL 1

Level 1 writing uses simple words and phrases that make sense and tell the story. Full stops are accurately used. Letters are well shaped and the correct way round, although the sizes may vary.

LEVEL 2

Level 2 is the level that the majority of children aged seven achieve. It is divided into three grades: Level 2A (highest), 2B and 2C, because it encompasses a wide range of performance.

Level 2C writing goes beyond simple statements of meaning. The ideas are given in short, complete units. The vocabulary used is suitable for the type of writing and may be narrative or non-narrative. The writing resembles spoken rather than written language. Common high-frequency words are correctly spelled; misspellings of unfamiliar words may show the writer has used knowledge of letter sounds to attempt them. The handwriting is generally legible although there may be some differences in letter size. Capital letters and lower case letters are mixed up within words.

Level 2B writing shows detail and variety in sentence structures and choice of vocabulary. It is organized for a purpose and the sentences may be longer, linked by words other than 'and'. Punctuation is used, though not always accurately. There is evidence of the writer successfully attempting unfamiliar spellings by use of knowledge of using letter sounds and patterns. Handwriting is clear and well formed.

Level 2A writing is lively and the meaning is clear. A style of writing is developing and the links between parts of the story or ideas are clear. Descriptive phrases may be used and there is a developing understanding of the use of punctuation such as capital letters and full stops to mark well-structured sentences. The spelling of many single-syllable words will be correct, with longer words showing the writer has successfully applied knowledge of letter sounds and patterns. Handwriting shows correct letter formation with clear ascenders and decenders on letters such as 'd' and 'g'. The letters are uniform in size.

LEVEL 3

Level 3 writing is clear in meaning and shows good organization and imagination. Ideas are developed logically and words chosen for appropriateness, variety and interest. Sentence structures are generally grammatically correct and spelling is usually accurate. Full stops, capital letters, commas and question marks are used correctly. Handwriting is joined and legible.

Examples of children's writing

To help you with assessing your child's writing, here are some examples of children's writing, with assessments. It will be clear from these that assessing a piece of writing is not easy. The assessment test is a subjective one, and opinions can differ when trying to assign a particular level to the work. To counter this in schools, the results given to the writing tests are checked and moderated by fellow professionals to ensure the best match for a level has been agreed.

As a parent or carer overseeing your child when she is attempting the Writing test, you will see how fluent and at ease your child is with the test. In this way you will get a general feel about her ability which will help you when you come to assess the writing to find the best match with a particular level.

Parent's
Booklet

Dadiscnetecf

Level W Here the writer spells a number of words correctly but has not yet grasped that each word is a separate unit. The letters have been formed with care, although the size and orientation are not always consistent. There is no attempt at punctuation and the meaning of the writing is not clear to the reader.

On Day my cat cot omos
and it ran unpr the beb and
my mum colud NOT FINd It
a nI wer and I crID.

Level 1 This story is written in a simple narrative form. It is a continuous sentence which begins with a capital letter and ends with a full stop. This shows an early understanding of the use and purpose of punctuation. The spelling of common words is accurate and the writer shows a good use of phonic knowledge to attempt words that she cannot spell. The handwriting is reasonably legible despite some poorly formed letters and a mix of capital and lower case letters in some words. Events in the story are linked by using the word 'and'.

one day my toth Fel out at skol
my mummy tal my to Pot it
under my Pilow.
Wen it was tdmto gow to bed
I heard a noys and sor sum
mone in my bed

Level 2C This story is structured and detailed, with ideas linked to give a flow to the writing. There is an attempt at dialogue, but overall the writing reflects spoken rather than written language. The handwriting is legible and, for the most part, well formed. Many of the common words are correctly spelled and phonic strategies have been used for spellings not known. Punctuation has been used to separate two events in one case but this is not consistent throughout.

Thomas and Amy are friends and they play on there bikes. one day Amy fel of her bike and hurt her leg. She stared to cry and Thomgs went to tell her mum. Her mum cam to look and wiped her leg. She gav them a Chocolate Biskit. They ate there bskit and played on there bikes agian.

Level 2B Here the writer starts by setting the scene. The style is consistent and meaning is conveyed to the reader. The story shows structure and is written in an interesting way. The writing follows the form of spoken rather than written language. The majority of the words used are correctly spelled and the handwriting is clear and legible. Although there is some inappropriate use of capital letters in some words, they have been used correctly for names. Punctuation is used to demark a number of the sentences but with some inaccuracies.

My space adventure

One day I went to the swing park. When I was there I saw a big shiny spaceship. I went inside and a mam sed I could have a ride. We wized of to a difrent planit were it was all blue and green. Wen I went home my freind didn't belive me. He sed is it tru?

Level 2A This story is lively and shows good use of vocabulary. It has pace and the reader is engaged from the beginning. Capital letters, full stops and question marks have been correctly used to demark sentences. The spelling of the majority of the words is correct and phonic strategies have been used for unknown words. The handwriting is legible and although there are some inconsistencies in letter sizes, the letters are for the most part correctly formed. A joined style has been used correctly for many of the words.

One lovely sunny day a boy went to the zoo with his mum. He went to look at the bears. One bear was all wite. "What sort of bear are you? he sed. The bear sed "I'm a pola bear and I live in the arctic were its cold and snowy. Please can I have a ice cream? but a notis sed do not feed the bears.

Level 3 This writing is detailed and imaginative with varied vocabulary. The events in the story are logically developed and the sentences are grammatically correct. The spelling is mostly accurate and the sentences punctuated correctly. The handwriting is clear and shows a joined style. The piece has pace with good use of descriptive writing.

THE SPELLING TEST

Follow the instructions given on pages 5–6 of the Test Booklet.

Dictation passage

The Farm Visit

Rose and **her** younger **brother**, Tim, live on a **farm**. They go to **school** in the nearby **town**. Every **year**, the headteacher arranges with Rose and Tim's dad, Mr Green, for a class visit.

The children always **enjoy** their visit. There are young lambs and calves to see, and Mr Green lets them **feed** the young animals with bottles of milk. The children can have rides on the **two** donkeys and give them pieces of apple and carrot.

There is an **old** tractor in the yard, and the children love to climb on it and pretend to **drive** it. Mr Green will not allow them to climb the hay bales stacked in the barn **because** it is too dangerous. The bales may **fall** and hurt the children or there may be **sharp** tools hidden in the bales that **could** injure them.

Mr Green shows the children all the machinery he uses for harvesting the **crops**. He explains how they work and tells them **about** how the crops were harvested in days gone by.

When it is time to leave, Mrs Green gives **each** child a small **cake** she has **made**. The flour she used was from the wheat they had grown last year.

Marking the Spelling test

If all the letters are present and in the right order, mark the spelling correct. Two marks are available for each correct spelling: award one mark for each correct initial letter, and one mark for each correct spelling of the whole word. Ignore incorrect use of capital and lower case letters. Ignore big spaces beween the letters.

Your child's answers will indicate whether she is aware of the sounds that make up words, and will reveal her knowledge of initial sounds and initial blends of letters such as 'cl', combinations of letters to make a sound such as 'ar' and common letter patterns such as 'ear'.

Answers to part 1 (pictures)

Question	Answer	Mark (initial letter)	Mark (whole word)
practice	tap	practice	practice
1	bowl	1 (b)	1
2	chair	1 (b)	1
3	clock	1 (ch)	1
4	dog	1 (cl)	1
5	plate	1 (d)	1
6	ball	1 (d)	1
7	glass	1 (gl)	1
8	jar	1 (j)	1
9	door	1 (pl)	1
10	spoon	1 (sp)	1

TOTAL 20 marks

Answers to part 2 (dictation)

Question	Answer	Mark (initial letter)	Mark (whole word)
practice	her	practice	practice
1	brother	1 (br)	1
2	farm	1 (f)	1
3	school	1 (sch)	1
4	town	1 (t)	1
5	year	1 (y)	1
6	enjoy	1 (e)	1
7	feed	1 (f)	1
8	two	1 (t)	1
9	old	1 (o)	1
10	drive	1 (dr)	1
11	because	1 (b)	1
12	fall	1 (f)	1
13	sharp	1 (sh)	1
14	could	1 (c)	1
15	crops	1 (cr)	1
16	about	1 (a)	1
17	When	1 (w)	1
18	each	1 (e)	1
19	cake	1 (c)	1
20	made	1 (m)	1

TOTAL 40 marks

Add up your child's total score, not counting the practice words. Enter the marks in the grid on the inside back cover of this book.